CONCERNS OF MORALITY IN LEGAL THEORY

Sesila Jata

Edizioni GRUPPO A.V. ITALIA srl

Bologna

Curatore Francesca Terrazzino

www.unavitadistelle.com

Part.Iva 03624001206, Bologna.

CONCERNS OF MORALITY IN LEGAL THEORY

SESILA JATA

THE CONTENT OF LAW AND ITS EXISTENCE: NATURAL LAW THEORY

''No more literature has been written on the concept of law than in any other field of knowledge [1] ." These words compose the first paragraph of Hart's most important opera, i.e. "The Concept of Law". In fact many legal theorists have filled the pages of philosophical and jurisprudential literature by trying to answer various questions such as what is law, how is law related to moral value, and what is the connection, if any, between law and morality.

During the eighteenth and nineteenth centuries law was presented as a 'science of principles'. Many jurists have tried to explain law as an expression of more abstract principles which may reflect necessary truths about the world and most of all human nature.

[1] Hart, The Concept of Law, Clarendon

The disputes between natural law theory and legal positivism are disputes regarding a n evaluative conception of law over a non-evaluative conception; more precisely, it is a dispute regarding the methods for the selection of basic jurisprudential concepts. John Finnis, a Natural law theorist of the twentieth century, explains "how the development of modern jurisprudence suggests that a theorist cannot give a theoretical description and analysis of social facts, unless he also participates in the work of evaluation, of understanding what is really good for human persons, and what is required by practical reasonableness." Thus Finnis engages in elaborating a set of basic goods that he claims to be self evident, with no need of demonstration. Shortly these basic goods are: "life, knowledge, play, aesthetic experience, sociability, practical reasonableness and religion". As we could easily understand Finnis avoid a metaphysics and transcendental recognition of God, forgetting the inadequacy of exceptionless moral norms to be foundations since also reason is one among the other equally basic goods.

SOCIAL PHENOMENA AND OBJECTIVITY

We could ask ourselve: is there any objective moral theory built upon ethical foundation that serves as the basis of any rational legal praxis. Has social scientist to become moral philosophers and both lawyers.

My opinion is that we cannot avoid some assumptions of value or morality and we must accept that social science must at some point judge or morally evaluate

So the debate between these two thesis as well described in all literature is based upon these two assumptions: (1) social science (for methodological reasons) cannot avoid moral judgments; and (2) that judgments of value, ethics or morality could exceed the role of science and rationality.

So, assuming that objectivity is quiet impossible to explain social phenomena we could prefer ‘enlightened social and cultural analysis’ to the 'simple prejudices' bound to relativistic assumptions. The absence of a moral basement for social science is a big inconvience, in my opinion.

Natural lawyers search for a moral principle by which to judge the validity of norms and for moral basis of legal authority and legal obligation .

The methodology of the natural science in the nineteenth century was an effort to model social science. Although it is true that social science has to depart from the methods of natural science in attempting to explain social phenomena, we should not abandon moral judgments in formulating its basic explanatory concept. So it has no need to abandon its aspiration to objectivity.

The theoretical struggle for the concept of law is a struggle for the concept of society itself, and that this is a philosophical aspiration.(2) The purposes of social science is to describe society as a normative structure, even though giving full recognition to the 'individual' in sociological explanation. To give an account of the nature of normative structure to society is to base our explanation on rationality, normalcy and pathology of normative institution.. That is to ground the normative structure of society in reason. We could say that the solution to the problem of the sociological explanation of norms is the solution to the Natural Law problem of the justification of norms.

In social science and ethics, objectivity and universal truth never have been, received with much enthusiasm. But we could also add that assumptions in Relativism have attempted to out–relativise previous relativism. This relativism is to be related to the issue of relationship between practical reason and cognition.

A smart solution to practical-moral problems, therefore, it is only possible within reason; and only if reason contains necessary and rationally undeniable, practical principles. Thus, we could also add that these practical principles can be consequences of the reflexivity of our constitution as practical beings.

Rationality is to be considered as the recognition that our practical interests shape our cognitive interests. In other words, we may conclude by the rejection of the notions of objectivity and truth..

Human actions and prescriptions can be interpreted in a variety of ways. Our needs condition our perspectives of interpretation. [2]Moreover this is an assumption of the relativistic view.

Anyway, practical reason is the organizing category of social theory. We may ask ourselves why we so fear the intrusion of moral judgment in our attempts to explain social phenomena. The answer could be that moral judgment precludes the possibility of objectivity; and objectivity is the definitive attribute of science. This is to assume that moral judgment and objectivity are mutually exclusive.

Objectivity and moral judgment should be reconciled in order to avoid problems for building a critical basis for social theory. The particular ends which may guide our lives, such as Finnis' theory of basic ends, can have conflicting interpretation between human beings. So we could call for Thomas Aquinas legal theory which basically

---

[2]This is a permissible reading of Nietzsche. E.g. Norris, in 'Deconstruction, where he says of Nietzsche's view on the Greek foundations of modern thought: "Behind all the big guns of reason and morality is a fundamental will to persuade which craftily disguises its workings by imputing them always to the adversary camp. Truth is simply the honorific title assumed by an argument which has got the upper hand – and kept it – in this war of competing persuasions."

affirms that “Law is a rational standard for conduct” and “it tries to achieve the final goal in life, which is metaphisical and transcendental. To give a moral reason to the concept of law is to choose a non arbitrary social theory based upon reason, although it may not be a sufficient condition. We may claim that the final goal is the reconciliation with God which leads to respect the principle of not harming anybody. That could be a common point of view between Natural Law theory and Positivism as conceived by its most important esponent, I. e. Hart.

These practical principle of not harming anybody derives essentially from a theory of substantive rationality. We should remember our nature as human beings thinking practically and being tied up by reason as the concepts of es, io e superio elaborated by Freud suggest.

LOOKING FOR THE FOUNDATION IN MORALITY: THE GOAL OF MORAL LIFE

We can see the topic of goal of moral life as a sort of ultimate goal meaning the sublimation of our impulses as human being which constitues our whole energy or libido as in Freud 'theory. It means that, within moral realisim we transform our energy in an intellectual work in the name of a virtuous life.

The goal of moral life in Aristotle' ethics is "Eudaimonia" (Happiness) as the final goal

I think that the goal of moral life is indirectly happiness, but first of all the self-realization of each human being as the final step of performance in life. Hence, Aristotle makes a hypothesis of a supreme end of human life and all its actions.[3] He assumes that the good life is founded on a vision of the best end of life. . This hypothetical end is called eudaimonia which should be characterized by perfection and self-sufficiency. This final end of human beings should be the first principle of ethics and is something realizable by human actions.

For Aristotle, the good is in the end on which everything else depends. These goods are arrived at by one's actions. By this, Aristotle confers a 'practical character' of the pursuit of the realization of the human goods. it is the supreme good for which everything else is chosen and lacks nothing. Happiness, thus, is superior to every other achievable good like honour, pleasure, virtue, etc. however, happiness could be viewed from another angle as inseparable and inclusive of all other goods.

We could affirm that it is clear that happiness consiting in self realization of human beings as the final destination of human life , is the general

---

[3]NE I, 2, 1094 a18-22: "If, then, there is some end of the things we do , which we desire for its own sake (everything else being desired for the sake of this), and if we do not choose everything for the sake of something else(for at that rate the process would go on to infinity, so that our desire would be empty and vain), clearly this must be the good and the chief good"

good, the general cathegory under which each of human beings can practice the basic good of self realization of identity.

The existence of an ultimate end is not an unreasonable hypothesis. Instead it conforms to an ontological status which therefore, rationally advance a hypothetical ultimate end of demands concretely human beings to act for a purpose. The definition of last end has happiness does not impose a unique mode of realizing it; it offers too different possibilities of pursuit of human goods. The first way is based on virtues. Aristotle conceives the pursuit of the last end of happiness according to moral virtues. But we should not forget the transcendental nature of human beings and their capacity to order themselves by virtuous acts.

The passage from Aristotle to Aquinas

Aristotle's superior being, God seems to be neither a moral nor a providential agent. It can be considered as an agent only in the sense of a final cause.[4] However God should be seen transcendent good to function as a foundation of morality. An inadequate account of God produces an inadequate account of human beings and their morality.[5]

As Freud says the core functioning of human beigns is based on irrationality, and religion is just one important aspect or impulse regarding Es.

It is impossible not to conclude the dependence of the natural law on the eternal law of God.

[4]'The Metaphysics', trans. Tredennick, London: Harvard University Press, I, 2, 983 a5-10.

[5]Rist, Real Ethics, rethinking the foundations of morality (Cambridge: Cambridge University Press, 2002), p. 148.

The goal of moral life in Aquinas' natural law ethics

The last end of human beings

Aquinas says that all human actions are for the sake of an end. They become human actions only by necessarily proceeding from the deliberate will. Morality can be said of only rational creatures who ''have dominion over their actions through their free will, which is the faculty of will and reason''.[6]

The general object of the will is the universal good. Human actions have a distinct end or purpose (telos), the achievement of which constitutes the completeness of human actions. There are two kind of order of end in human actions: the order of intention and the order of execution. The principle of intention is the last end which moves the rational actions. But if we look at it from the point of execution, the first principle is the first of the things which ordained to the end. And if something has to begin, it has to have an end as a last end to which the will moves through its means. The chain of ends cannot proceed in infinitum. So Aquinas

[6]Summa Theologica, trans. Fathers of the English Dominican Province, Allen – Texas: Christian Classics Publishers, 1981, I-II, q.1, a.1.

concludes that there is an ultimate end. However, the human will cannot be directed to many ends as last ends at the same time.

It is for the fulfillment of the last end that all human beings desire and it is precisely in this fulfillment that happiness consists, or in other words self-realization.. According to Aquinas there is no dispute at this level of generality. '' but as to the thing in which this aspects is realized, all human beings are not agreed as to their last end."[7] The last end that constitutes the true good of human being is to be found in God

[7]ST I-II, q.1, a. 7.

Ordo rationis: a requisite to realize the last end

. The happiness of an active life can be lost when someone choose vice instead of virtue or when adverse circumstances inhibit the performance of virtuous acts.

For pursuing happiness, rectitude of the will is necessary. Rectitude of the will is the right order of the will to the last end. It is a disposition of human reason. It is characterized by a series of virtuous acts, which are ordered, according to priority, to the ultimate good. '.We can remind Socrate's words about the maximum pleasure leading to a virtous life by just making a simple calculation of interests. A virtous life is the best of human beings especially if it translates into an intellectual or other kind of work men ca realize for their seilf realization as the final step of their purposive life.

The rectitude of Human Will in Order Rationis

As the natural things have their species from their forms, so too, the actions have their species from their objects.

The action is to be good if all circumstances, object and the ends are good. '' If the good of man is to be in accordance with reason and evil is to be against reason, then good and evil of human acts are predicated in reference to reason. If it is so, then the goodness and wrongness of moral objects will effect a difference of species making the act to be good or evil. Sometimes, a circumstance is taken 'as the essential difference of the object, as compared to reason; and then it can specify a moral act."

Aquinas further distinguishes two aspects of voluntary action: the interior act of the will and the exterior act each having its own objects. While " the exterior action takes its species from the object on which it bears, [so] the interior act of the will takes its species from the end, as from its own proper acts." So, the species of a human act can be considered formally and materially. The formal species is considered from the end and material species from the object of the external action. For example, when one steals to commit adultery, formally he is not a thief but also is an adulterer although he is only a thief speaking of the species of object of the act.

If a circumstance becomes a principal condition of the object, then it can determine the species. ''a circumstance added to the object that specifies the action, can again be taken by the directing reason, as the principal condition of the object that determine the action's species". Any circumstance , for that matter, which becomes the principal condition of the object, should specify the act ''. A circumstance can give the species of good or evil to a moral action, in so far as it regards a special order of reason."[8]

Right reason is the principle of moral acts of its goodness and badness. The good or evil in the act of the will is derived properly from the object of the act which is presented by the reason. If the object is in accordance with reason, it enters into the moral order and causes moral goodness in the act of the will. The principle of goodness and malice of human actions come from the interior act of the will. Then the goodness of the will should depend on the object of the end and not on the circumstances..[9] In Aquinas, for an act to be good, it must be good both in relation to the end and in relation to its matter and circumstances.

As the interior act of the will and the external act are morally considered one single act, so too their goodness, if it is considered from its relation

---

[8]ST I-II, q.18.

[9]ST I-II, q.19.

to the end. However, if the external action considered from its matter and circumstances , it can have a distinct goodness from the interior act. However, they affect each other's goodness and combine to form one act in the moral order. The external action by itself cannot change the goodness or the malice of the interior action unless the agent wills it. However, it can add the goodness or malice of the will. The consequences cannot make either a good action evil or an evil action good. However, the goodness or malice of action can increase or diminish if the consequence foreseen or if they are not foreseen but follow from the nature of the action itself. The accidents and side effects do not enhance or diminish the goodness or malice of an action.[10]

[10]ST I-II, q.20.

ORDO RATIONIS AS THE FOUNDATION OF NATURAL LAW ETHICS'.[11]

God is the last end of human life. All human acts and goods are ultimately chosen to realize this last end. All other human goods either basic or instrumental are subordinated to this transcendent good. The recognition of this transcendent or absolute good provides an objective valid moral direction. Basic goods are valid reasons, self-evident (per sé) to human subjects which function as guidelines and standards for human actions.

But basic goods could be considered sometime arbitrary and subjective, and reason cannot avoid urges and passions that characterize human beings. Simply calculation of interests maybe is not sufficient. Consequently the criterion of ordo

[11]ST I-II, q.69

rationis should consist in ordering human acts and goods to realization of the last end, the union with God. This could constitute the first principle of morality for the choice of human acts. Reason does not justify the pursuit of basic good since we are to be considered as irrational beings.

The plenitude (fullness) of human subject concerns the realization of his faculties and powers which are expressed in his activities. So, it is through the operation of the human acts which are directed to God as the last end that a human person can achieve his plenitude of goodness. Consequently, if morality is rightly pursued in human acts and human goods, one should adhere strictly and completely to the absolute criterion of ordo rationis to realize the plenitude of being. Schultz reports that according to Aquinas, without the first desire of this last end, there cannot be specific human inclinations or any particular objects of attraction. It is this rational desire for the last end that should conduct and govern all other desires and inclinations. Once this desire for the ultimate end is established and rationally defined, this can orient and direct all human desires, urges, inclinations, passions and choices of acts and goods to the realization of the fullness of one's being.

THE QUESTION OF GOD

There could be two possible versions of natural law theory: theistic and secular. If it is theistic, God as the last end of human beings has the supreme role and all acts and human goods are ordered to God. Both types of theories can rely on reason to enumerate the basic goods. However, the lists of such human goods can vary on the basic as to whether the reason recognized the existence of God or not. If God's existence is not affirmed as in secular interpretation, it will be no mistake to pursue natural happiness. But, if he does exist, then, it will be absurd to bracket him out of a moral theory.[12]

Aquinas' natural law doctrine is based on the existence of God as a major premise of his

[12]Rist, Real Ethics, p.153

arguments. Aquinas provides a theory of morality founded and ordered to God, the final goal of human life. [13] What is relevant for morality, however, is an order of human acts and goods towards a worthy fulfillment of one's being which is achieved only in realizing union with God, the last end. However, this does not imply that morality does need to inquiry into the nature or the essence of God. That could be investigated in theology or in metaphysics. Thus, Rist concludes: ''for morality to function , God must function both as final end and (at least in great part) as efficient cause of moral life''.

Since we are irrational beings we need a credential moral foundation without losing the final causality, which could be only God. Moreover, we should not forget the inviolability of basic goods and the exceptionless moral norms to have in this way an objective moral theory.

The history of morality has seen different moral criteria and corresponding moral orders. The criterion of utility in utilitarianism, passion in Human, autonomy and freedom in the modern

---

[13]Rist, ibid., p. 155-6, Finnis and his group of analytical philosophers will dissent from Aquinas on this point.

theories, proportionate reason in proportionalism and the criterion of practical reasonableness in the new natural law theory, etc., have not provided a sound criterion for an objective moral order. Thomistic morality alone has conserved an objective criterion of the ordo rationis which is developed from Aristotelian roots. Both Aristotle and Aquinas seem to move from an objective moral order characterized by an objective moral criterion of right reason to a moral agent who is called to realize the ultimate end, union with God and is endowed with capacities that transcend the person himself towards the ultimate.

A CRITICAL APPRAISAL OF FINNIS' NATURAL LAW THEORY

The last century abounds in theories of human goods.

Proportionalist theories are merely 'teleological' and seek to base moral judgment in the attainment of the best state of affairs. Kantian theories, on the other hand, are called 'deontological' and are 'duty oriented' which endeavour to ground moral judgments in the universal rationality of the moral agent.

Finnis begins his moral investigations in human experience and not in an abstract concept of human nature or in divine command. Rather, he shows how moral norms are rules of action are derived from a human experience of desires and inclinations and not from the static notion of essence or human nature.

Some actions to be intrinsically evil. consequently Finnis could cogently propound the absolute prohibition of intrinsically evil acts. These immoral and unnatural acts are morally forbidden without any exception. The intrinsically evil acts, which Finnis prohibits exceptionlessly are acts which violate the basic goods. However, this notion is indefensible since inviolability of basic goods is without a rationally adequate moral foundation.. the inviolability of basic goods is not accounted for.

Basic goods of the new natural law theory

Finnis understood the difficulty of proposing a single basic good as a categorical imperative for deriving moral norms.

Most of the criticism of the new natural law theory are centred on the notion of basic goods: on their choice and on their nature. There seems to be some kind of arbitrariness involved in their choice.

The basic goods are self-evident for those wise teachers who have experience life. It is this self-evidence of basic goods which is the foundation of morality in Finnis. As the belief of self-evidence is apprehended only by the wise and the learned, Finnis cannot be justified to speak of a morality for all persons.

Moral Goodness and Moral Rightness

In proportionalism, a judgment on the moral rightness of the act is made not based on the conformity of the act to right reason but on the proportion of the good or evil effect. The act would be wrong only in the evil it contained outweighed the evil it contained. As such, an evil act could be done for a greater good. What is at stake in this moral reasoning is the goodness of the interior will which can be good only if all aspects of the human act are good. In their ambition to found an objective morality based on a scale of proportion, proportionalist neglected the central axle of morality, viz., the person and the interior will. The emphasis transferred from the acting person to the act, from the moral goodness to the rightness, from the interior act to the external act. Instead, for Aquinas, the goodness of badness of the exterior act precisely depended on the goodness of the will of the interior act. For Aquinas, the external act could be bad either by reason of its intention or by reason of what is willed. This means that an act could be bad apart from a good intention (i.e., proportionate reason for the proportionalists).

The movement from the First Principles to Specific Moral Norms

According to Aquinas, the very first precept of natural law is : ''bonum est faciendum et proseguendum et malum vitandum." In addition to this, there are other prima et communia principia legis naturae such as the Golden Rule or ''evil is to be done to no one". The specific moral norms form the third grade of principles, which are moral precepts concerning actions, ''which are necessary for observance by the more discriminating consideration of reason by those who are wise".

These are principles ''whose meaning is not evident to everyone but only to the wise Aquinas has not specified or ordered the movement from the first principle of practical reason to specifical moral norms clearly and coherently perhaps because he was writing in an age of faith.

Sidelining of Moral Virtues

Aristotelian and Thomistic philosophies recognized the importance of the virtues for a good moral life. Precepts and virtues are two aspects of the same morality. all moral laws whether negative or positive make the acting subject good. The negative precepts guard one from moral evils and the positive precepts exhort the interior will to incline to do good. In either way, the effect of the law makes the acting persons good. . In Aquinas, moral virtues inwardly dispose persons rightly towards the basic ends and, thus, rectify the human practical reason in its pursuit of imperfect beatitude. For Finnis, it is the integral human fulfillment which is the object of rectified human reason.

Human fullfilment is possible only by virtous act. Practical reasonableness is not sufficient since we are irrational beings.

The Hidden Role of Nature

If the existence of God is not necessarily as a foundation of natural law theory, then what justifies the basic goods in Finnis? Finnis seems to have them justified in human nature. He states : ‘’the diversity of the basic goods is neither a mere contingent fact about human psychology nor a accident of history. Rather, being aspects of the fulfillment of persons, *these goods correspond to the inherent complexities of human nature*.”[14]

We cannot avoid ethics and virtue as notions corresponding to human nature since it is requested by our constiitution, by Superio in Freud theory.

[14]Finnis, Practical principles, p.107.

Rationalistic theory

Finnis' new natural law theory looks more like a rationalistic than a rational theory. There could be various reasons for this. A rationalistic system of ethics seems to presuppose a society consisting in well-balanced individual who are not affected by fate, chance, evil, etc. None of these effects the person in theory.

Also history has a role in plasming our needs for the fullfilment.

MORALITY IN LEGAL POSITIVISM

THE DIVIDING LINE BETWEEN NATURAL LAW THEORY AND LEGAL POSITIVISM

The analysis of law is kept strictly separate from its evaluation. Modern legal positivism developed in reaction to certain (less sophisticated) versions of natural law theory. John Austin wrote what has become perhaps the most frequently cited summary of legal positivistic ''dogma'': ''The existence of law is one thing; its merit or demerit is another. Whether it be or be not is one enquiry; whether it be or be not conformable to an assumed standard, is a different enquiry. A law, which actually exists, is a law, though we happen to dislike it, or though it vary from the text, by which we regulate our approbation and disapprobation".[15]

Positive law has a role within moral thought and moral practice. Positive law plays a crucial in achieving social/common goods that require the deployment of state power or the coordination of citizen action. If what makes one a natural law theorist is adherence to a certain kind of metaphysical realism about morality[16]--natural law theorists seem to agree that moral realism is an important component of the tradition, but disagree on the extent to which the tradition requires other significant commitments.

Similarly, if natural law theory reduces to the claim that there is objective moral truth, and that this truth should be used to evaluate our political and legal institutions as well as our individual choices, and legal positivism reduces to the claim that there is a possibility of and value to a descriptive or conceptual theory of law separated from any evaluation of its (moral) merits, then

[15]Austin, The province of jurisprudence determined, 1995.

[16]"Moral realism" has been defined as "the view that moral beliefs and judgments can be true or false, that there exist moral properties to which moral agents are attentive or inattentive, sensitive or insensitive, that moral values are discovered, not willed into existence nor constituted by emotional reactions"

there would seem no reason why one could not support or advocate both. Indeed, a number of prominent legal positivist and natural law theorist have so claimed at one time or another. For e.g. Hart, has described Finnis's natural law theory as being ''in many respects complementary to rather than a rival of positivist legal theory". And Raz, in 'The Morality of Obedience', has claimed that ''it is a mistake to think that the legal positivist and the natural law traditions are inherently incompatible".

Hart had offered an important development of legal positivism in particular, and of legal theory in general, when he argued that theories of law should take into account, and indeed be built around, the perspective of a participant in the legal system—to be grounded on the meaning that aspects of the system have to those participants, as contrasted with taking the quasi-scientific perspective of a complete outsider.[17]

Finnis agrees with the importance of constructing theory around an internal point of view, but he suggests amendments to the view-

[17]Hart, the Concept of Law, (emphasizing the importance of an internal perspective in the course of analyzing habits, rules, and law).

point selected by Hart. Hart uses the viewpoint of the participant who ''accepts'' the legal system, in the sense of using the legal rules as the criteria for guiding and appraising his own behavior and the behavior of others, but Hart took a broad view of the nature and motives of such ''acceptance''. Finnis suggests that this central viewpoint be narrowed to that of the participant who is following the law because (and thus, only when) the law imposes (presumptive) moral obligations of obedience and whose judgment on these subtle moral questions is good. He states: "One internalizes the law when one willingly, promptly, readily—and not merely out of extrinsic motivations of fear of punishment or hope of reward—complies with its requirements, not only according to the letter of the law but primarily according to the lawmaker's intention and plan for common good. Such states of affairs are the central case of law because they most fully instantiate the fundamental notion of law: a prescription of reason, by means of which rational and indeed conscientious and reasonable practical judgments about the needs of a complete community's common, public good, having been made and published by lawmakers, are understood and adopted by citizens as the *imperium* of their own autonomous, individual practical reason and will."[18]

In other words, morality is important in determining what the positive law should be.[19]However, this is a far different claim from stating that one could use morality to determine or describe what the positive law of a particular legal system currently is.

Legal positivists usually present their dogma about the separation of law and morality in terms of separating the attribution of legality or legal validity from evaluation of the legal rules' or legal system's moral worth. 'What both Bentham and Austin were anxious to assert were the following two simple things: first, in the absence of an expressed constitutional or legal provision, it could not follow from the mere fact that a rule violated standards of morality that it was not a rule of law; and, conversely, it could not follow from the mere fact that a rule was morally desirable that it was a rule of law.'[20]This view of legal positivism, and of

---

[18]Finnis, Aquinas: Moral, Political and Legal theory, 1998.

[19]Finnis, Natural Law and Natural Rights, p.281-90.

[20]Hart, Essays in jurisprudence and philosophy.

its difference from natural law theory, is connected to an equation of natural law theory with the phrase, ''*lex iniusta no est lex*''. The expression is true, and indeed somewhat banal, when understood as saying that unjust laws are not laws ''in the fullest sense,'' in that they do not create moral obligations to obey them in the way that just laws do.[21] Finnis wants to transform our discussions of legal positivism and the separation of law and morals. He urges that natural law theorists have never denied a disjunction between positive law and moral merit and that *lex iniusta*, properly understood, never claimed the contrary.[22]

A theory of little value, significantly inferior to theories which have such moral content. Finnis initial small-scale challenge regarding the best way to construct the internal perspective of a legal system can be seen as a challenge to the legal positivist position in this sense. If a theory that does not morally evaluate its internal perspective is markedly inferior to a theory that does, then a non-evaluative approach to law may be possible, but it is of little value.

[21]Finnis, Natural law and Natural Rights, p. 363-66.
[22]Finnis, ibid., (accepting the disjunction of legal validity and moral evaluation).

The legal positivist response to the morality-centered criticism has often been to advocate the importance of the objective or (social) scientific perspective. In responding to another prominent critic of legal positivism, Ronald Dworkin, Hart puts forth the following argument:" There is a standing need for a form of legal theory or jurisprudence that is descriptive and general in scope, the perspective of which is not that of a judge deciding ''what the law is," that is, what the law requires in particular cases...but is that of an external observer of a form of social institution with a normative aspect, which in its recurrence in different societies and periods exhibits many common features of form, structure, and content."

Hart's point is that moral analysis within and about the law may be useful and important, but such importance does not negate the value of looking at the law from the point of view of social science.

However, it is important to note that while Dworkin may deny the value of a social science or social theory approach to law, it seems clear that Finnis does not oppose such an approach. He has made clear on a number of occasions that a ''descriptive social science of law,'' derived in part from Weber and Aristotle, facilitates a clear discussion of the nature of law. Finnis's complaint against Hart (and other legal positivists) is not that one should not attempt a general social theory of law, but rather that one should not expect such a theory to be non-evaluative.

Finnis's view is that law should be understood in connection with the moral ideal to which it is aspiring and the moral function it is intended to play. One cannot fully understand a reason-giving activity unless one understands what it would take to make something a good reason for action. Lon Fuller, in the context of discussing the later treatment of evil actions validated by Nazi law, wrote of ''the dilemma as that of meeting the demands of order, on the one hand, and those of good order, on the other.'' From Fuller's other writings it seems clear that he might add that it is difficult to understand the idea of ''order'' without having a clear notion of what ''good order'' is.

This is where the issue between legal positivism and natural law theory may be finally joined, though the battle lines will never be entirely clear. Finnis has been an important figure in discerning where the true dispute lies between natural law theory and legal positivism. He has developed the argument that law can only be understood in a moral-based teleological analysis. This is substantial challenge, one that hits at the core of legal positivism, and it will be interesting to see what responses legal positivism can offer.

HOW MORAL PRINCIPLES CAN ENTER INTO THE LAW: THE IDENTIFICATION OF LEGAL NORMS

There are many ways in which law and morality interact. Legal positivist have somehow denied the consistence of important law-morality connections.

There are some debates between exclusive legal positivists on the one hand and inclusive legal positivists and incorporationists.

Inclusive legal positivism consists in the following thesis: it can be the case, though it need not be the case, that a norm's consistency with some or all of requirements of morality is a precondition for the norm's status as law in this or that jurisdiction. While such a precondition for legal validity is not inherent in the concept of law, it can be imposed as a threshold test under the Rule of Recognition in any particular legal regime.[23] That test, which can be applied by the officials in such a regime to all of legal norms therein or to only some subset of those norms, is one of the criteria which the officials use for ascertaining the law. Some degree of moral worthiness is a necessary condition for the legally authoritative force of each norm that is validated as a law within the system. Inclusive legal positivism, which readily accept the possibility of such state of affairs, is inclusive because it allows that moral precepts can figure among the criteria that guide officials ascertainment of the law. An inclusive legal positivist insists that such tests are contingent features, rather than essential features, of the systems of law in which they are applied.

Incorporationism, instead, consists in the following thesis: it can be the case, though it need not be the case, that a norm's correctness as a moral

---

[23]Hart, The Concept of Law, (The phrase Rule of Recognition refers to the array of criteria that empower and obligate the officials in a legal system to ascertain the existence and contents of legal norms in accordance with standards specified by those criteria , which are largely- if not exhaustively-ranked. The Rule of Recognition in any legal system is a framework of normative presuppositions that underlie the law-identifying behavior of the officials in the system.).

principle is a sufficient condition for its status as a legal norm in this or that jurisdiction. That moral principles regularly regarded by officials as legally determinative are indeed legal norms, notwithstanding that they have perhaps never been laid down in any explicit sources such as legislative enactments or judicial rulings. So incorporation of moral principles is contingent

Exclusive legal positivism maintain that the very nature of law is inconsistent with the role of moral principles as legal norms and with their role as criteria for validating legal norms. Those principles are extra-legal standards. Such standards effect the decision reached by the official but only because those decision are not based solely on legal requirements.

Each of them as a distinctive variant of legal positivism has developed in reaction to Dworkin's early critiques of H. L. A. Hart.[24]

Hart had happily acknowledged that the criteria for law-ascertainment in any particular legal system can include moral principles. He had

[24]Dworkin, Taking rights seriously (Cambridge, MA: Harvard University Press, 1978).

chiefly in mind criteria that constitute restrictions on law-making power.

The role of moral precepts as law-validating criteria or as legal norms, the Exclusivists have denied that moral precepts can play any such role. In other words, they have sought to rebut the Dworkinian challenge by arguing that moral principle cannot enter into the law; Joseph Raz is the leading advocate of this Exclusivist position,

Scott Shapiro, a defender of Exclusivism, has propounded , . Incorporationists maintain that the Rule of Recognition in any regime is conventional, and they further maintain that the conventions involved can take any number of routes.

Shapiro argues that, when officials adhere to an Incorporationist Rule of Recognition, the legal norms which they ascertain and invoke are not reasons for the decision which they reach. Instead, those reasons reside wholly in the Rule of Recognition itself. . At most, the formulations of the principles are explications of what is already required by the Rule of Recognition.

A non-Incorporationist Rule of Recognition, by contrast, does indeed engender laws that are themselves reasons for officials to reach certain outcomes as opposed to others. Under the criteria in such a Rule of Recognition, correctness as a moral principle is never sufficient to qualify a norm as a legal norm., Each legal norm constitutes a partly independent reason for an official to arrive at the rulings which the norm requires.

Shapiro contends that the distinction between the incorporationist and non-incorporationist rules of recognition is of the utmost importance because of the basic role that is ascribed to law by Hart and most other legal positivists: the role of presenting people with norms that can guide and direct their conduct. Moral principles validated as laws under an incorporationist rule of recognition cannot supply the requisite guidance. Legal norms that do not constitute any independent reasons for or against specific decision are thereby devoid of any capacity to affect the balance of reasons that will confront the officials who might invoke the norms. Officials whose reasons-for-action derive from R1 do not gain any further reasons-for-action from the correct moral principles which they apply thereunder. they likewise cannot perform any such role in connection with the behavior of ordinary citizens. the moral principles validated as laws under R1 will present the citizens with no reasons-for-action that have not already been presented to them by R1 itself. As reason-giving guides to conduct, then, those principles /laws are utterly redundant.

Such is the gist of Shapiro's critique of Incorporationism. INSTEAD inclusive legal positivism runs afoul of the same general difficulties that based incorporationism. The claim made here is not that a rule supposedly validated by an inclusive rule of recognition that made morality a necessary condition on legality cannot make a practical difference. The problem is that such a rule cannot make a practical difference in the way that rules are supposed to make practical differences.'

Everything is fixed from the outset, so long as that Rule of Recognition endures. And precisely because the contests and implications of the legally incorporated moral principles are fixed from the outset, those principles themselves do not furnish any additional reasons for officials to arrive at certain decision. Nor do they furnish any additional reasons for citizens to adjust their behavior in certain ways.

The Conventionality of Law

Any Rule of Recognition is best understood not as a coordination convention but instead as a constitutive convention. That is, the law-ascertaining criteria in a Rule of Recognition are not a solution to some pre-existing problem of getting certain people to align their patterns of behavior; rather, those criteria constitute a social practice within which any number of distinctive values and objectives and problems develop.

Though that constitutive conventions are prone to change, whereas coordination conventions tend to be much more stable. some other constitutive conventions such as the rules of chess are generally very stable, whereas some coordination conventions such as ordinary language are susceptible to numerous mutations.

According to Marmor, constitutive conventions are necessary if people are to have reasons to carry out the various steps that amount to participation in the activities which those conventions have shaped. In the absence of such conventions, people would have no reasons to perform those steps (such as the moving of chess pieces in certain ways).

This line of reasoning by Marmor is question-begging at best, and is thus wholly inconclusive. Marmor would in turn contend that his opponents are abandoning their adherence to the notion that law is essentially conventional.

But One could accept that every legal system is a product of constitutive conventions, while also affirming that any such system can contain some laws that would be binding as outcome-determining mandates even in the absence of the conventions that form the system in which they exist as laws.

To insist on the conventionality of law is not perforce to concede that the conventionality must invariably be it consists in sundry convergent modes of behavior Albeit the principles validated as laws by an incorporationist rule of recognition are not themselves conventional qua precepts of critical morality, their status as laws is indeed conventional through and through in the senses just delineated. That status would cease to obtain if the rule of recognition were to change in certain ways because of alterations in the behavior and attitudes of the relevant officials.

For the very same determinations. Nevertheless, in regard to each official, the concertedness of the behavior of other officials is indeed a factor that militates in favor of his going along with them by employing incorporationist standards for the ascertainment of laws. The concertedness is a sufficient reason for him to do as they do.

On Uncertainty

For example, Eleni Mitrophanous,[25] a steadfast supporter of Raz, observes that a crucial function of a legal system is to reduce sharply the uncertainty that would prevail in the absence in such a system. She infers that the criteria in any rule of recognition must 'secure certainty in the identification of laws' and she contends that those criteria as understood by inclusivists or incorporationists would not be capable of achieving adequate certainty. While acknowledging that not all moral matters are controversial and that not all factual matters are uncontroversial, she submits that the inclusion of morality in the law would very likely generate an unacceptable level of uncertainty that would thwart the fulfillment of law's function. She allows that 'the question is one of degree', and she asks 'what the degree of uncertainty in the identification of law can be tolerated by a consistent

[25]Mitrophanous, Soft Positivism, 1997.

incorporationist or inclusive legal positivist'. ... offers no argument for a screening process to avoid uncertainty'.

BIBLIOGRAPHY

- **"Legal Positivism", Mario Jori, 1992,Dartmouth**
- **"Rationality, Social Action and Moral Judgment", Stuart Toddington,1993,Edinburgh University press**
- **"In Defense of Legal Positivism, Law without Trimmings", Matthew H. Kramer,1999,Oxford University press**
- **"Jurisprudence or Legal Science? A Debate about the Nature of Legal Theory", Sean Coyle and George Pavlakos,1988,Oxford and Portland, Oregon**
- **"Philosophy of Science, the Central Issues", Martin Curd, J.A. Cover, Christopher Pincock, W.W. Norton e Company**
- **Specific Absolute Moral Norms in John Finnis An Assessment", Rinoy Joseph 2003**
- **"The Law of Peoples", John Rawls, 1999,Harvard University press**
- **"Justice as Fittingness", Geoffrey Cupit,1996,Clarendon press**

- **“Autonomy and Rights, the Moral Foundation of Liberalism”, Horacio Spector,1992, Clarendon press**
- **“Current Legal Problems 1999”, M.D.A. Freeman,1999, Oxford University press**
- **“Legge naturale e diritti naturali”, John M. Finnis,1996, G. Giappichelli Editore**
- **“Where Law and Morality Meet”, Matthew H. Kramer,2004,Oxford University press**
- **‘’Natural Law and Natural Rights”, John Finnis,1980, Oxford University press**
- **‘’Notre Dame Law Review”1612 1999-2000**

www.ingramcontent.com/pod-product-compliance
Ingram Content Group UK Ltd.
Pitfield, Milton Keynes, MK11 3LW, UK
UKHW022010190726
13853UKWH00004B/1846

9 791280 619068